What To Do
WHEN YOU
DON'T KNOW
What To Do

Published by Blue Angel Publishing
80 Glen Tower Drive, Glen Waverley,
Victoria, Australia 3150
E-mail: info@blueangelonline.com
Website: www.blueangelonline.com

Edited by Susan McLachlan

Blue Angel is a registered trademark of Blue Angel Gallery Pty. Ltd.

ISBN: 978-1-922161-55-0

What To Do
WHEN YOU
DON'T KNOW
What To Do

44 WAYS to be Calm & Clever
When Life Gets Confusing

Alana Fairchild

BLUE ANGEL®
PUBLISHING

Life can get confusing. Even with a positive attitude and a courageous heart, sometimes you will feel uncertain. How should you deal with the curveballs life throws your way?

When life gets confusing and you feel like you are lost at sea, this helpful little book will be your life raft, keeping you afloat, guiding you back to dry land.

Just take a deep breath, relax and open the book randomly at a page. You'll get your answer. And you'll know what to do.

Relax

WHEN YOU ARE WORRIED OR STRESSED, your body and mind get tense. Without even realising it, you will stop breathing deeply and maybe even start holding your breath. These unconscious reactions to stress just make things seem worse. Focus now on taking a slow, deep inhalation and then a slow, full exhalation. This is how you relax. Relaxed bodies and minds cope with challenging situations much more easily than those that are stressed out. You are also going to find a solution to any problem more quickly when you are calm.

Do
Something
Different

IF YOU WANT TO FEEL DIFFERENT,
then do something different. When you can't see a way
out of a confusing dilemma, it's time to shake things up!
Even if you start with one change to your daily routine,
that's enough. When we do something different, we set
a different outcome in motion. Remember that insanity
is repeating the same thing and expecting a different
outcome. Change some of the ingredients in the recipe of
your life and you can transform it from sour to sweet.

Walk Away

SOMETIMES THE BEST WAY
to gain peace of mind and a better perspective is to get
some distance. Step back. Try to stop thinking about the
situation for at least a few hours. If it is practical to take
a longer break from dealing with the issue, at least a few
days, then do that. When you have some distance,
you can look at the situation more objectively, perhaps
from a higher perspective, and the best choice to make
becomes clear.

Laugh

YOU MIGHT THINK YOU SHOULD

only laugh when times are good, but you need laughter even more when times are difficult. Don't be afraid to laugh when life gets challenging. Laughter releases feel-good hormones into your body and when you feel good, it's easier to have a positive attitude. A positive attitude is going to help you see a solution. A negative attitude will stop you from believing that there is a solution. You'll think it is hopeless and give up trying. That's not going to get you very far. So find a way to laugh instead. A laugh a day keeps negativity away.

Don't
Be A
Hero

EVERYONE NEEDS HELP SOMETIMES.

It isn't weak to ask for help, it's smart. We can get further in life when we help each other. Don't be a hero and think that you have to sort out a problem all on your own. What matters is that the issue gets sorted out and it will be easier for that to happen if you let people help you. But don't expect the people in your life to be mind readers.

Ask for what you need – a shoulder to cry on; a good listener; someone to motivate you to take action; or some good, practical advice for health or finance (or whatever relates to your challenge). Ask for help from friends. Visit a counsellor, a healer, a mentor, a financial planner, a coach, a lawyer, your bank manager. If you feel your pride getting in the way, think how much more proud you'll be when the situation is finally sorted out. If you don't know what you need, or who to ask, then it's time to call in the "big guns." Go outside. Stare at the sky. Say out loud, "Universe, please help with …. I am so grateful for the excellent solution you are already sending my way. Thank you!" Ask and you shall receive.

Don't Judge A Book By Its Cover

WHATEVER CHALLENGE,
crisis or confusion is happening in your life, there is
something good that is trying to come out of it. *Every*
cloud has a silver lining – even the dark, stormy, scary-
looking clouds. The hidden blessing trying to get to
you through whatever is happening in your life will be
revealed at the right time. Remember, rainbows can
only happen when it rains. When things seem dark and
stormy, trust that it's going to work out and it's going to
be *good*. Always keep some hope in your heart.

Choose To Feel Happy

DO YOU BELIEVE THAT HAPPINESS
is a "special occasion" emotion? That you can only feel it when something really good happens, like a wedding, or a promotion, or when you fall in love, or a child is born? Happiness is meant to be an everyday emotion. You might feel even more happiness when something special happens, but you can still feel some happiness every day if you choose to do so. Once I saw a butterfly flying in the rain. It was so beautiful, bright and cheerful. I wondered how it kept fluttering so lightly out in the downpour, but it did. Happiness is like that butterfly. A butterfly doesn't only exist on sunny days. It is still a butterfly when it rains. It still flutters joyfully even when skies are grey. You don't have to save up your happiness for a special occasion or a sunny day. Today is one day closer to the solution to any problem you are having. Things are going to work out anyway. So why not choose to be happy whilst they do?

Go Back
In Time

ONCE UPON A TIME, YOU WERE A CHILD.

You were curious and open to learning new things. You questioned everything, probably testing your parents' patience with your much-repeated question, "Why?" You had loads of energy. You giggled at dragonflies and saw faces in the clouds that moved across the sky, even when the boring adults around you didn't seem to notice the magic in life. When you are feeling tired, mentally blocked or locked in indecision, you need to connect to the child within. There is a wise solution to every problem in life, but to find it, sometimes we need to stop trying to work everything out like a sensible adult. There is a saying, "out of the mouths of babes," which refers to that moment when a child says something incredibly wise and perceptive. We might not expect that a childlike attitude can help us figure out what to do, but children are curious and open to learning something new. When what you already know isn't helping, you need to learn something new so that you can find a solution. The child within will help you do this. So get in touch with your inner child. What did you like to do as a child? Play in nature? Stare at the sky? Curl up with a book? Colour in pretty pictures? Dance in your lounge room? Do that.

Work Smarter, Not Harder

WHEN YOU DON'T KNOW WHAT TO DO, it's time to make two separate lists. The first list is called, "Things I can control." That will include choosing your attitude, expressing yourself honestly and any other practical actions that you can realistically accomplish. Do what's on that list. The second list is called, "Things I cannot control." That will include other people's reactions, and exactly how and when things sort themselves out. Do not try to do anything on that list. Remind yourself that whenever you try to control something (or someone) that you cannot control, you are wasting your energy. If you focus on what you can control, and put all your energy into that, you are working smarter rather than harder.

Break
It
Down

YOU DON'T EAT A MEAL WITH ONE HUGE BITE.
You don't need to solve a problem with one action either.
Break down the problem into bite-sized pieces. Think of
simple steps that you can do one at a time. Make a list of what
you can do today, over the coming week, or even over the
next month or so. What positive, practical steps can you do
today? Can you ask for help from a family member, friend or
professional adviser? Can you make a call, have a conversation
that you need to have? Prepare yourself mentally with positive
thoughts? Take care of yourself emotionally and physically
with good nutrition, enough exercise and rest? Do you need
to get some more information or some advice – legally,
financially, or on a health matter? Practical steps will help you
feel empowered, gain confidence and work your way towards a
resolution, one step at a time.

Let Go
Of The Past

AFTER YOU HAVE DONE ALL THAT YOU CAN DO, even if just for today, it's time to let go. Disappointment and regret are only meant to be temporary squatters in the house of your soul. They will help you learn to do things differently next time. If you allow them to take up permanent residence in your heart, you'll become unhappy. Instead of learning from your mistakes, you'll be beating yourself up, trying to change the past, which is something that cannot be done. Learn from the past, but don't hold on to it. If you need to forgive yourself or someone else, do it. The only thing you'll get from holding on to the past is fatigue because it takes energy away from the here and now. When you let the past go you can transform the pain of your past into energy in this present moment.

Be A
Water Baby

A WALK BY THE OCEAN.

A swim. A bath. A shower. A foot bath. Rinsing your wrists under cool water. An icy drink on a hot day. A hot cup of herbal tea on a cold day. There's a reason why we offer a guest in our home something to drink, especially a cup of tea, if something stressful has happened. Water is healing, cleansing and soothing. It refreshes body and mind which makes it easier to recognise a calm and clever solution for any of life's difficulties.

Pay It
Forward

THE UNIVERSE WANTS TO BRING

all sorts of good things into your life. You just have to know how to receive them. To receive, we have to learn to give. Or another way of putting it is that you get what you give. Some people call this karma but that can sound a bit punishing, and the Universe doesn't want to punish you, it wants to *help* you. So you might prefer to think of it this way instead. The Universe is like a mirror. It reflects back to you what you give out, so the best way to receive a helping hand in your own life is to do something nice for someone else. Help someone randomly. A kind gesture, word or smile will do the trick. So will sharing some information, saying a prayer for someone else who seems to be doing it tough and asking the Universe to help them out. Do this without expecting how the help will be returned to you. Just know that it will come.

Become More Spiritual

BEING MORE SPIRITUAL DOESN'T MEAN
becoming impractical, sticking your head in the clouds and
forgetting about day to day matters. It means feeling more peace
in your heart because you trust that there is a loving intelligence
that is looking out for you. That loving intelligence might be the
Universe, God, the Goddess, the angels or you might not even
be sure who or what is out there and that's just fine. Simply being
willing to believe that there is a greater plan unfolding in your
life is enough. Sometimes it will feel loving. Sometimes it might
feel more like tough love. But either way, you trust that somehow,
even when you don't understand or feel in control, things are still
working out according to a greater purpose. Then you'll realise
that you don't have to be in control for things to work out perfectly.
All situations resolve themselves so much more easily when you
trust.

Keep Your Eyes (And Ears) Open

BE OPEN TO RECEIVE A SIGN.

There's no such thing as a coincidence. If you feel like you are being given a nudge to do something, pay attention. Different people telling you the same thing could be your sign. Noticing some words on a billboard as you drive down the street might be your nudge from the Universe. I once saw a sign out the front of a church that said, "If you are looking for a sign, this is it!" Even a line in a movie or a book that you are reading might jump out as significant for you. The Universe is always giving you signs, guiding you, trying to help you out. Signs are a bit like love. If you try to force them to happen, they generally won't. But if you relax, you'll loosen up and find that love is everywhere. So to recognise the signs that the Universe is sending your way each and every day, just relax, look and listen.

See That Glass
As Half Full

QUANTUM PHYSICS DEMONSTRATES
that when you change the way you look at things, the things
you look at change. You can use the power of your attitude to
make things better or worse. If you want to feel good and find a
solution, it makes sense to use your power for good! Become a
radical optimist. Put a positive spin on everything. If you don't
know how something can be positive, choose to believe that
something positive will come of it later on, even if you can't
see that yet. A negative point of view is not realistic. A negative
point of view is not practical. A negative point of view is not
going to prevent disappointment. A positive attitude will help
you in ways that you might not realise until you try it. So why
not try it? The only thing you're going to lose is your negative
energy – and your life will be so much better without that!

Be
Grateful

WHEN YOU DON'T KNOW WHAT TO DO,
be grateful. The Universe is giving you a gift. Consider it
to be like a little holiday, where you take your hands off
the steering wheel and allow the Universe to take over
for a while. Have a snooze. Enjoy the scenery. You may
want to take action, but when you feel as if your hands
are tied or you feel that trying to sort something out at
the moment may just make matters worse, then drop
it. Enjoy cruise mode. Soon enough it'll be your turn to
take the wheel again. For now, why not enjoy being in the
passenger seat for a change?

Speak Up

WRITE A LETTER TO THE UNIVERSE.

Express what you feel and what you hope for. Ask for the best possible solution to something that is troubling you. Don't be shy. Ask for what you want clearly and without shame, because you know that your words will be answered. Remember to say "thank you" at the end of your letter. Once you have finished writing your letter, sit down and become focused. Forget about everyone else for a few moments and let this be your time. Read your letter aloud, as if you are reading it to the Universe. Speaking aloud is powerful natural magic. You have that magic, that power, within you. Don't talk about the things you don't want to happen. Speak positive words. Use your power wisely.

Prepare
For The
Unexpected

HAVE YOU EVER HEARD THE EXPRESSION

that life is what happens while you are busy making other plans? Or how about the one that says if you want to make God laugh, tell him your plans?

There are two things that you can expect in life. Firstly, there is always a solution to any and every dilemma. Secondly, and more often than not, the solution will not be what you expected. Anything can happen! Some people get nervous about the unexpected. They think it means that something bad will happen. That negative attitude is not true or wise. It will make you unhappy and fearful. A great opportunity could come right to your door, but you might not accept it because you are afraid. What if people laugh at you? What if you make a mistake? What if this, what if that? Then you make it hard for life to help you out. You can teach yourself how to be more optimistic. When opportunity comes knocking at your door, you can respond with positive thoughts like, "Something good is going to happen and I am ready for it!" That sort of positive attitude cuts through problems like a knife through butter. The right solution will find you more quickly, as it will be unable to resist your enthusiastic heart.

Trust
Your
Instincts

WHEN YOU DON'T KNOW WHAT TO DO,
trust your instincts. Imagine you are a surfer. You work
hard to paddle out to sea, then you have to be patient and
sit on your board for a while, learning to sense which
wave is going to give you the ride of your life. When it
comes, you paddle like crazy to catch that wave and you
enjoy the ride so much you cannot help but shout with
joy. People watching you are inspired! When you pay
attention to life, you'll sense when you need to wait and
when you need to act. You'll sense when there is a great
opportunity heading your way and you just need to go
for it. Trust what you feel and you'll know when to be
patient and when to paddle like a pro-surfer.

Turn A Mountain Into A Molehill

PERSPECTIVE CAN TURN YOUR STRESS DIAL RIGHT DOWN.
Think about a bigger problem than yours for a moment. Maybe it's a difficulty that someone you know is having, or even a global problem affecting people who live in poverty or in war zones. Don't make yourself depressed, but do give yourself a reality check to put what is happening in your own life into perspective. Then say a prayer to the Universe, "Please help the people who are suffering get the help that they need as quickly as possible." Then say, "I am so grateful that my problems are so much smaller. Please help me to solve them too."

You'll calm down, realise that your problem is not as huge as you once thought, feel more positive *and* give out some positive energy to the world too.

Drop Some Love Bombs

LOVE IS POWERFUL.

It is a magnet for good things, including inspired solutions, to come into your life. Doing something loving for yourself, for an animal, or for another person, strengthens the magnetic field of your heart. This field has been measured in scientific studies. These studies have shown that the heart is much more powerful than your brain. Love is literally smarter than you think. When you act from your heart in a loving way, even if it doesn't seem to directly relate to an issue you are trying to resolve, it will help you to attract the right people, answers and situations into your life – and anything else you might need too. Act on love's behalf, and love will act on your behalf.

Listen To Your Body

OFTEN, NOT KNOWING WHAT TO DO
is a sign of overwhelm. Do you need to eat? Do you need to rest? Do you need to drink some water? Do you need to cool down or warm up? Or maybe you just need to take a well-earned break. Listen to your body. If you are overwhelmed and trying to think clearly, it can feel like trying to meditate in the middle of a rock concert! There's just too much going on. When you do something nice and calming for your body, your feeling of overwhelm will quieten down and you'll find that your mind becomes clearer too. Then it's easier to hear the answers within.

Be At
Peace

PEACE IS ALWAYS A CHOICE –

even when things are going crazy around us. If you choose to trust that things will always work out somehow, then you'll find it easier to feel peaceful. When you feel peaceful, it's a bit like picking up a telephone and calling God or the Universe for a chat. Peace opens up a channel of communication with a higher and loving intelligence, making it very easy for this higher intelligence to place answers in your heart. They just slip right in there, without you even realising it at the time. Later the answer will occur to you, as if "out of the blue." It will probably seem so obvious to you that you might wonder why it took you so long to work it out. Or maybe you'll think you are so clever because it's such a great solution! Either way, you'll have your answer. So be at peace. Put yourself in a place where you find it easier to be peaceful. Perhaps it will be a pretty parkland; the beach; an almost empty church; or closer to home you could have a candle-lit bath and listen to some relaxing music as you tell yourself in a gentle, soothing voice that you are safe and everything is going to be OK. Believe it. Give yourself the gift of peace.

Be
Impressed

WHEN YOU DON'T KNOW WHAT TO DO,
you are outside of your comfort zone. This is the place
where personal development and spiritual growth
happen. It is also where your life can change for the
better. You can only discover new things in life when you
are willing to go through unfamiliar territory. So what if
you don't know if you are coming or going, which way is
up, and which way is down? Be impressed with yourself!
You are growing. This is good. You are travelling through
unknown territory and you'll find something new and
improved will come into your life because of that. Be
excited. Be proud.

Get Your Mind Right

WHEN YOU GET YOUR MIND RIGHT,

it becomes your friend, rather than your enemy. Your mind can be the voice of encouragement that helps you to keep going until you get what you want. It can also be the voice of doom, making things seem far worse than they truly are; conjuring up nightmarish situations that won't ever happen, but that still manage to frighten you. When your thoughts make you feel fearful or depressed, it's time to get your mind right. Start by choosing not to over-think things. The best solutions to any problem are usually pretty simple. If a situation seems to be getting complicated, your mind is probably getting in the way. Learn how to settle and soothe your mind. In a calm voice, like you were speaking gently to a child, say to your mind, "I know you are trying to keep me safe, but you don't have to worry anymore, because everything always works out just fine." You'll be teaching your mind to feel relaxed rather than frightened. Fear creates tension, awkwardness and pain. The more relaxed your mind is, the more easily you'll be able to move through life's ups and downs. It can take some time and patience for your mind to learn something new, so don't give up on yourself. Getting into a daily habit of being kind and optimistic with yourself is the way to get your mind right.

Choose Which Voice To Listen To

WE EACH HAVE A VOICE OF LOVE

and a voice of fear within us. You might think of it as your shoulder
devil and your shoulder angel, or even two wolves inside of you –
one that would destroy you and one that would protect you. The
voice that we choose to feed with our attention is the one that grows
strongest. Even though the voice of fear might be more familiar,
it is not more truthful. In fact, the voice of fear will tell you many
lies. It will say you can't trust anyone or anything, that things are
always going from bad to worse, and that you have to fight against
life because it is unfair and cruel. The voice of love is what you are
listening to when you have hope and trust in your heart and you
know that everything is going to work out according to a greater
plan. The voice of love protects you from the negative influence of the
voice of fear. It actually makes your life easier and more enjoyable.
So be smart. Sometimes you might hear the voice of fear, but you can
always choose to *really listen* to the voice of love.

Be Willing
To Wait

COOKING CAN BE A WAY TO FILL YOUR BELLY
with a nourishing meal and also teach you something about life.
We all know that you have to break a few eggs to make a cake. This
means that for something good to happen, there will typically be
some chaos and mess first. Once you do what you can and finally get
that cake in the oven, you have to wait. Cooking needs time. Just like
life. If you try to force something to happen more quickly by turning
up the heat, you'll end up with a burnt cake and have to start over
again. Sometimes you just have to wait and that will be quicker than
trying to make life happen faster. In the same way that the oven timer
will always eventually ring, so too will things come together in your
life when the time is right. So cooking teaches us two important life
lessons. We don't need to be scared when things get a little messy and
with a little patience, things will come together at the right time.

Feel A
Little Crazy

WHEN LIFE SEEMS OUT OF YOUR CONTROL

and you don't know what to do, there will be moments when you may wonder if you are simply losing your mind. Most people in this world are afraid. They think that if they trust life a little more and try to control things a little less, something terrible will happen. When you are doing the very thing that most people around you try to avoid, they'll likely believe you are nuts. Some days you may wonder if they are right! Just remember that there is a big difference between feeling a little bit crazy and actually going crazy. When you feel like you are losing your mind, what you are actually doing is choosing your heart over your head. You aren't going insane. You are choosing love instead of fear. You are letting go of needing to control everything and instead you are learning to trust. You are just learning to live in a way that will make your life easier, happier and healthier in the long run. People who think you are crazy for doing this don't understand that the really crazy behaviour is to live in a way that makes you afraid. Living in fear isn't fun or helpful at all. It holds you back from so many wonderful choices in your life. So there's no need to panic. It's absolutely OK to feel a bit crazy. Sometimes that's just what being brave feels like.

Birds
Of A
Feather

THERE'S AN EXPRESSION THAT GOES LIKE THIS –

"If you lay down with dogs, you'll wake up with fleas." Another way to say it is that spending time with negative people can make you feel negative. You might wish them well, but you won't want to make these people your regular companions in life. Hang out with people who are smart enough to be excited about the challenges in life, who see them as opportunities for positive change. Don't have people like this in your life yet? Read inspirational books. Attend a weekend workshop, a free seminar or enrol in a course. Be open to positive energy and positive people in your life. If people are bringing you down, then step back. You need positive energy to be brave, and if you want to live a good, loving, exciting life, you'll need to be brave! Negative energy saps your courage and dulls your spirit. Choose to do things that make you feel positive and you'll start to attract more positive, like-minded people into your life. As the other expression goes: "Birds of a feather flock together."

Be Good
To Yourself

IT CAN BE TEMPTING TO BLAME YOURSELF
when you feel like you have lost control of your life. Don't
fall into the trap of feeling stupid, like a failure, guilty, angry,
unworthy or ashamed. You are better than that. Respect
yourself. You are doing a great job. Life delivers the big
challenges to those who can handle them. You'll work it
out. The Universe will help you. Trust yourself and trust
the Universe. In the meantime, be aware of what you tell
yourself. Encouraging words and validation are going to give
you energy to keep going until you get through the situation,
and make the whole experience not only quicker, but less
painful too. Then you can congratulate yourself on how
clever you are under pressure!

Believe In The Impossible

WHEN YOU CANNOT SEE HOW A SITUATION can possibly work itself out, it's time to start believing in the impossible. You can be like the Queen of Hearts in *Alice in Wonderland* who likes to believe in at least six impossible things before breakfast. It's not only in the world of stories where the impossible becomes possible. Impossible things happen in our world every day. We only considered them impossible until they were accomplished. Mountains have been climbed, aeroplanes have flown, computers have become smaller than your hand and rockets have been launched into space. What we think is impossible is just something possible that hasn't happened yet. Your "impossible" solution will happen too. Have a little faith.

Shine
A Light
On It

MOST OF US HAVE THE HABIT OF AVOIDING THINGS

that we fear. We don't even stop to think clearly about what the fear is, we just feel it and run. We can do this physically by avoiding situations that seem challenging, but we can do it with our minds too, by not giving ourselves a chance to really understand what we fear and figure out if it's real or not. It's a bit like dreading a monster in the wardrobe, but never opening the wardrobe to see for certain what's in there. Imagine all the suffering you would save yourself by opening that wardrobe door and having a look inside. You might worry that expressing your fear is being negative. But if you express your fear and then respond to it with a calm and soothing voice, you can take what was negative and transform it into a positive. Fear can make you feel paralysed. When you confront it, you feel better, stronger, more confident and more energised. That's a lot of positive from one negative! To shine a light on your fear, be willing to look closer. Write a list entitled, "What am I afraid of?" Don't be ashamed. Everyone has fears. When we write them down some of them may actually seem quite silly. Some will seem serious. No matter how silly or serious those fears seem, you need to respond to each and every one on your list. Let yourself know that it is most unlikely that those fears will ever happen. Fear can seem real, but more often than not it is just a symptom of exhaustion in your body or mind. Sometimes the best response is to reassure yourself that no matter what happens, you'll take care of yourself. You've managed to do that for this long and you'll keep on doing it. Then deal with the real issue at hand and get some rest.

Hips Don't Lie

DANCE.

Whether you are out in public or in the privacy of your home, whether you share the moment with others or close your eyes and make it all about you. Switch on some music and shake your hips. To feel better, you need to express yourself, not repress yourself. Forget about how it looks. You might close your eyes and hardly move at all, but you could be dancing wildly on the inside! What matters is how it feels. Dance is when you get to communicate through your body what you may not be able to put into words. If you don't try to control how you move and just let it happen, dance becomes an honest and freeing conversation between you and your body. So let your body speak. Trust your hips, your hands, your arms, your feet. Listen to yourself. You might just learn something. And have some fun doing so.

Spring Clean Your Soul

WHEN YOU FEEL CONFUSED, CHAOTIC OR OVERWHELMED, you simply have too much going on. You are overloaded psychologically, and maybe even physically, too. It's time to Spring Clean your Soul and offload some unnecessary burdens from your shoulders. What can you clear out of your life? Be ruthless! Treat yourself like you would treat your best friend. Be in your own corner and support yourself to make some tough love decisions. Are you taking on too much? Can you postpone some commitments or just say no? Do you allow certain people to take advantage of you or do you feel drained and exhausted after spending time with certain people? Those sorts of relationships aren't respectful. If you are going to respect yourself, you'll cut such people from your life and look after your own needs for a change. Spring is in the air! Don't be afraid to clear out what you don't need anymore, so you'll be ready for something new (and improved).

Shhhhh!

SILENCE CAN BE A SOOTHING REMEDY FOR CONFUSION.
In the modern world silence is rare and often so unfamiliar that people might be scared of it at first, as if being left alone with their thoughts is like being locked in a dark closet with a monster! But silence is like an unusual food with high nutritional value. You might have to develop a taste for it, but once you do, you'll start to crave it because it's just really good for you. In modern life, there's so much noise, pollution, information and even electro-magnetic fields constantly streaming at us. It's no wonder that we sometimes feel frustrated or overwhelmed, even if we cannot find a particular reason for it. It gives new meaning to the expression "I can't even hear myself think!". When there is a power failure, one of the first things I notice (after the location of the nearest torch) is how peaceful I feel. When all that electricity has been switched off, there is more stillness and quiet. I relax more deeply without even trying. All the noise and activity of life can be exciting, but there is a point when it can become a bit too much. In such cases connecting with silence can discharge an overloaded mind and replenish the body. If you don't want to wait until the next power failure to feel it, why not find yourself some quiet time in another way? Do a miniature version of an electricity black out at home and switch off your mobile and email for half an hour, light some candles and just relax with a cup of tea. Or turn your bathroom into a sanctuary of soothing quiet with only the sound of the shower water rushing over you or the lapping of bath water helping you to wash away worry and clear your confusion. If you can't get any peace at home, get out into nature or go to a place that tends to be quiet and reflective - like an art gallery or museum. In silence, the quiet voice of inner intuition can be heard so much more easily. The answers you need in life are already within you. Sometimes you just need a little quiet time to be able to hear them.

Write
Your Future
Story

THERE'S A SAYING THAT WHEN WRITING THE STORY OF YOUR LIFE, you shouldn't give someone else the pen. What do you want to happen in your life? Start acting as if that, or something even better that you can't imagine yet, is what *will* happen. Hoping for the best but expecting the worst can be like praying for what you don't want. If you like the idea of making a vision board with images that make you feel good and capture the future that you want to experience, do that using pictures from magazines or that you download off the internet. Or write a story about your future, and what it's going to be like, according to your hopes and dreams. Then focus on the *feeling* of your best-possible imagined future. Can you imagine how happy you'd be feeling, how safe and content, how excited and fulfilled, or loving and peaceful? Do whatever you can in your life now that makes you feel those same sorts of feelings. Get yourself into the emotional habit of feeling those feelings whenever you can by focusing on what makes you feel those things. Writing a 'gratitude list' can be a way to do this. Today is the day that you are writing the story of your future. You write it with your feelings, your thoughts, your choices and your imagination. It's your story. You get to write it anyway you'd like. Why not make it the best one you can imagine?

Sing

IN THE CAR WITH THE WINDOWS UP OR DOWN, in public, in the shower, singing feels good. It releases stress. It makes you smile (and possibly makes other people smile too if they catch you bursting into song whilst driving). Singing encourages you to breathe deeply and has similar effects on body and mind as exercise. The ancient spiritual traditions from India teach that singing activates creative power and helps you get organised, set priorities, gain energy and solve problems. All that from singing along to the radio? Yes please! So open your mouth and let some sound out.

Change Your Shoes To Change Your Views

MY GRANDMOTHER USED TO SAY THAT TO UNDERSTAND another person, you need to walk a mile in their shoes. Hollywood gives us a spin on this idea through 'switching identity' movies where through some unusual turn of events, two people end up swapping bodies for a while. The mother lives as the daughter and vice versa, or a man and woman in a relationship switch bodies, living each other's lives for a time. In those films, two people come to understand and love each other better when they have had a chance to learn what it's like to live as that other person for a while. They come back to their own lives with more wisdom because they've had a chance to look at the world through another person's eyes. They learn that there was actually more to life than their own initial viewpoint. We might not have a chance for a real-life version of such Hollywood fare (quite possibly a good thing as I suspect it would be rather more entertaining on screen than in reality!) but we can do a less dramatic (but just as helpful) version of it by considering the old expression 'two heads are better than one'. Ask for another person's view on an issue. Be willing to see something through a different set of eyes. Different view points can help us see situations from another angle, taking into account aspects of a situation that we might not of even considered previously. That can be enough to help us come up with a different approach to an issue. And maybe even see an opportunity where once we only saw the obstacle.

Smell
The Roses

SCENT ACTIVATES THE LIMBIC SYSTEM
in the brain, stimulating an emotional response. Studies have shown that a pleasant scent improves mood and increases a sense of wellbeing and a positive viewpoint. Incense, aromatherapy oils, perfume or even pleasing aromas from the kitchen can shift your mood from blue to a more pleasing hue. Take time to smell the roses, and you'll see the world through rose-tinted glasses too.

Hug It Out

HUGGING LOWERS STRESS HORMONES,
fights fatigue, boosts the immune system and fights
infection, and stimulates production of feel-good
hormones. Hugging makes you feel happier and
improves your health. Hugs work best when you feel safe
and trusting, so unless you feel particularly comfortable
with hugging a stranger, choose to hug a loved one, a pet,
or even yourself! Got arms? Hug it out!

Plan Your Pleasure

DO SOMETHING THAT BRINGS YOU PLEASURE.
There can even be pleasure in planning it, if needs be. Eat
a delicious nourishing meal or get together with loved
ones. Watch a film or curl up with a good book. Indulge
in a candle-lit bath or get a massage. Or all of the above!
Pleasure can help relieve stress in an enjoyable way.
As Mary Poppins says, "a spoonful of sugar helps the
medicine go down."*

*"A Spoonful Of Sugar" is a song from Walt Disney's 1964 film and the musical
versions of Mary Poppins, composed by Robert B. Sherman and Richard M. Sherman.

Do Sweat The Small Stuff

SWEAT IT OUT TO WORK IT OUT.

Exercise will clear your mind and reinvigorate your body. Don't feel like you have time to exercise? Then you probably need it even more. Studies have shown that apart from physical health benefits, exercises boosts creativity, productivity, energy levels *and* problem solving skills. So stop thinking and start moving your way towards an inspired solution.

Shelve It

DO WHAT YOU CAN DO NOW

and don't worry about what you cannot do right now.
A popular technique to help people relax is to ask them
to leave their worries on a shelf. They can collect them
again after the relaxation exercise is over, if they wish, but
for that moment, they can simply put them aside. You
may even find that once you let go of your worries, you
manage well enough without them. You can leave them
on the shelf. Permanently.

About the Author

ALANA FAIRCHILD may not have met you yet, but she knows you. She knows that inside you is a beautiful, wise and strong being. She wants you to remember that, to trust yourself, and live a life you love, from the inside and on the outside too. If you want to find out more about Alana and her work, join her online:
www.alanafairchild.com

Notes

Notes

Notes

Notes

For more information on this
or any Blue Angel Publishing release,
please visit our website at:

www.blueangelonline.com